A Joshua Morris Book
Published by The Reader's Digest Association, Inc.
Copyright © 1994 Victoria House Publishing Ltd.
All rights reserved. Unauthorized reproduction,
in any matter, is prohibited.
Printed in Hong Kong.
Library of Congress Catalog Card Number: 94-66822
ISBN: 0-89577-645-6
2 4 6 8 10 9 7 5 3 1

WILDLIFE HOMES

NATURE SEARCH

Author
NEIL MORRIS

Consultants
PROF. MARTYN MURRAY
DR. WILL CRESSWELL

Illustrators
NEIL BULPITT   DAVID HOLMES
BRIN EDWARDS   EVA MELHUISH

a Joshua Morris book
from The Reader's Digest Association, Inc.

CONTENTS

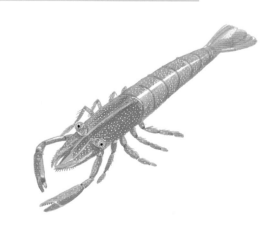

HOW IT WORKS

WILDLIFE HOMES

Animals make their homes in all kinds of places, from trees and caves to mounds and burrows. Enter this world full of surprises and color, and discover all the wonderful places that different animals call home. Some creatures are hidden or camouflaged – use your magnifying glass to search the different habitats and see what you can find. Look for this magnifying glass symbol. It indicates which creatures you should look for.

There are other challenges to test your powers of observation. For instance, you'll find an owl nesting in a very unusual place!

There are answer pages at the back of the book as well as a glossary, where you can find out about the creatures that appear on every page.

DESERT SHELTER

It is sunrise in the Arizona desert. The ground is already getting hot, and the dry air blows gently over the rocks. Most animals are getting ready to shelter themselves from the fierce heat. The pack rat and the kangaroo rat retreat into their burrows. The jackrabbit does not live underground but heads for the shade of a nearby cactus.

The cactus plants are home to many birds. A cactus wren is watching out for her eggs. Higher up in the giant saguaro cactus, woodpeckers have made a hole for a nest. Nearby, a roadrunner is catching food to feed its chicks, while a thrasher perches near its nest on a spiny cactus. Overhead, a kestrel hovers as it surveys the desert scene and searches for prey.

Reptiles, such as the desert tortoise and the gila monster, are cold-blooded. They come out of their homes in the morning so that the sun can warm their bodies and give them more energy to move around.

CAN YOU FIND THEM?

Many desert animals are small and well camouflaged. Using your magnifying glass, can you spot these creatures?

There may be as many as six coyote pups in a litter.

This elf owl lives in a woodpecker's abandoned home.

Curve-billed thrasher chicks are safe in their spiky home.

Sand crickets have bristly legs to help them burrow.

The black racer snake can easily climb a prickly cactus.

The tiny yucca moth lays it eggs on yucca flowers.

DECORATING THE NEST

Pack rats build nests of twigs and dry grass. Then they pick up and bring home bright-colored objects and pieces of litter. Can you see what this pack rat has found?

HIGH-RISE HOMES

The noise is deafening! These cliffs, high above the Atlantic, are crowded with colonies of seabirds. Echoing off the rock walls, their harsh cries fill the air.

Many of these birds spend most of their time at sea, coming to land only to breed and raise their chicks. Puffins and lesser black-backed gulls rest on the cliff tops. Kittiwakes and fulmars build their nests on rocky ledges. Guillemots don't make nests for their eggs at all. The female lays a single egg on a bare cliff ledge. Guillemot eggs are pointed at one end so that, if moved, they roll in a circle and not over the cliff's edge.

Lower down, razorbills nest on broader ledges. Shags and cormorants build nests of seaweed on big ledges and flat rocks. All of these birds must watch out for herring gulls, which ruthlessly plunder unguarded nests for eggs and chicks.

From behind the cliffs, a peregrine soars into view. The peregrine is the fastest of all falcons, and it hunts other birds in flight. Even birds as large as the gulls are wary when a peregrine is nearby.

BURROW NESTS

Puffins nest under the ground in burrows. Sometimes they use empty rabbit burrows and make a hollow inside, or they make their own burrows using their large bills as shovels. The female puffin usually lays a single egg inside the burrow, where it is safe from gulls.

CAN YOU FIND THEM?

The eggs and chicks of seabirds are well camouflaged. Using your magnifying glass, can you find these eggs and chicks?

Fulmar chick

Guillemot chick

Kittiwake chick

Kittiwake egg

Razorbill egg

Lesser black-backed gull egg

Guillemot egg

Razorbill chick

RIVER HOMES

In springtime, this European river is full of life. The birds have finished building their nests and are hunting for food. A penduline titmouse visits its home high in the branches of a tree. Kingfishers live in holes in the riverbank. One of them perches patiently, waiting to dive for small fish. A goosander and a coot have also left their nests to swim and look for food.

A muskrat is diving for water plants and fish. Like the water vole, it nests in a burrow in the riverbank.

Dragonflies lay their eggs in water, and their young stay submerged until they are fully grown. Frogs and newts lay eggs in the water too, and these hatch into tadpoles.

A male stickleback protects the female's eggs in their underwater nest from enemies like the bream.

LEAVING THE NEST

Goosanders are fish-eating ducks. They nest in a tree hole near the river.

When her ducklings are big enough, the mother pushes them out of the nest. The young goosanders have to jump to the ground, which is often several feet down. Then their mother leads them to the river.

CAN YOU FIND THEM?

See if you can spot these tiny creatures with your magnifying glass.

The ramshorn snail likes water with plenty of water weeds. It eats tiny plants as it crawls along.

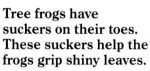

Tree frogs have suckers on their toes. These suckers help the frogs grip shiny leaves.

The caddis fly larva lives in a tubular case that protects its soft body.

The water vole nests in a burrow in the riverbank.

Female newts lay hundreds of single eggs on the leaves of water plants.

The diving beetle is a ferocious hunter. It will attack frogs and fish.

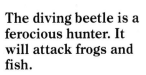

LEDGES AND CRAGS

High in the Himalaya Mountains the air is thin and cold, even in late spring. Lower down, the rhododendrons are in bloom. Here there are few trees, but there are lots of meadows and colorful mountain flowers.

Himalayan mammals have thick coats to protect them from the fierce winds and severe cold. They find shelter where they can in the rocks. Brown bears sleep during the winter months in dens they make in cave holes or among boulders. In spring, the female nurses her cubs in the den. The marmot makes a burrow and a cozy nest of dry grass.

Other animals hide from their enemies among the rocks. The ibex, a wild goat, climbs along the ledges to the highest crags. During the day, the small musk deer lies hidden from hunters like the snow leopard. Only at dusk will the musk deer venture out to feed.

SPLITTING BONES

The lammergeier, or bearded vulture, lives in a big nest near the cliff's edge. It feeds on dead animals, even eating the marrow inside bones. Lammergeiers split open the bones by dropping them onto rocks from a great height.

CAN YOU FIND THEM?

Birds build nests in hard-to-find places so that the eggs and chicks will be safe. Using your magnifying glass, try to spot these nests.

The lammergeier lays one or two eggs in its large nest of sticks.

Using sticks and dry roots, the alpine chough makes its nest in overhangs in the cliffs.

The wall creeper nests in rock crevices, plastering over the entrance with mud.

The rock nuthatch nests in crevices in the rocks.

The alpine accentor makes a cup-shaped nest of grass roots, mosses, and lichens.

15

SPOT THE DIFFERENCE

Every year the rainy season comes to the jungles of Brazil. The Amazon River rises and floods huge areas of land. The birds that live here make their nests high above the water. Macaws and toucans nest and raise their young in tree holes. Smaller birds, such as crested oropendolas and yellow-rumped caciques, weave hanging nests. Hummingbirds build tiny nests beneath the leaves.

Vampire bats live together in groups. They do not build homes but roost in trees during the day. Orb spiders also live in the trees. They spin webs across the branches and wait for flying insects to become trapped.

A leaf-cutter ant carries a piece of a leaf back to its nest, while a tree frog sits waiting to catch passing insects. Tree frogs spend most of their lives clinging to twigs and branches with the suction pads on their feet.

Other animals, such as the anaconda and the caiman, swim around looking for food. The black caiman sleeps at the water's edge. The giant otter lives in a burrow in the riverbank.

There are six differences between the picture above and the one below. Can you spot them all?

A CLUSTER CAMP

Army ants have no permanent home. They move constantly through the rain forest, eating insects and other animals. When they rest, they form a huge cluster inside a hollow log or underneath a branch. They hook their legs together, and the closeness of the ants' bodies creates their own shelter.

MOUNDS AND BURROWS

Rising out of the flat grasslands of Africa's Rift Valley is a huge mound, the home of a termite colony. Soldier termites guard the mound; workers make the tunnels, build the walls, and grow a food-substance fungus on beds of chewed leaves. The queen and her king are at the center of the mound.

The termite mound is a center of activity for many animals. The dwarf moongoose digs in search of a meal. The scaly pangolin uses its sticky tongue to catch the termites. A lilac-breasted roller bird perches on the mound, waiting to catch bees and locusts.

Nearby are other animal homes. The flat tortoise is perfectly shaped to fit into crevices in the ground. Banded mongooses post guards to watch over their burrows, looking out for enemies like the martial eagle, which can swoop down on them from a great height.

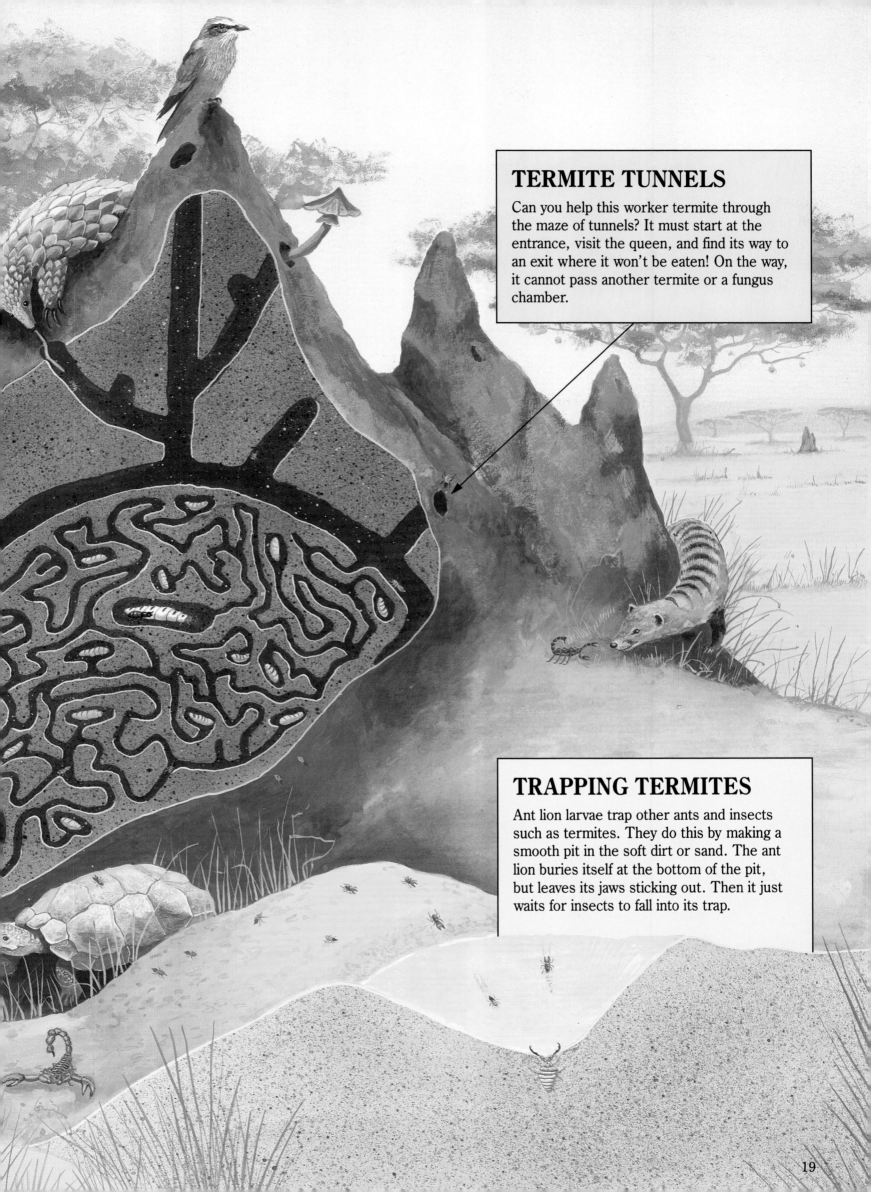

TERMITE TUNNELS

Can you help this worker termite through the maze of tunnels? It must start at the entrance, visit the queen, and find its way to an exit where it won't be eaten! On the way, it cannot pass another termite or a fungus chamber.

TRAPPING TERMITES

Ant lion larvae trap other ants and insects such as termites. They do this by making a smooth pit in the soft dirt or sand. The ant lion buries itself at the bottom of the pit, but leaves its jaws sticking out. Then it just waits for insects to fall into its trap.

LIVING IN THE SEA

The Red Sea is a long, narrow arm of the Indian Ocean. Deep in its waters a wealth of animals depend on each other for life. The big humphead swims among the corals, feeding on smaller fish. But it does no harm to the cleaner wrasse, and even allows the smaller fish to swim safely into its mouth. There, living up to its name, the cleaner wrasse rids the humphead of parasites by eating them.

The remora hitches rides on bigger creatures, such as turtles. The clown fish is able to hide among the sea anemones because it is not hurt by their sting. In return, the clown fish attracts other kinds of fish, thus bringing food to the anemone. Soft coral gobies sometimes share their homes with shrimp. The shrimp make a burrow, and the gobies guard the entrance.

Cowries take their homes with them. They are sea snails with egg-shaped shells. Four of them are crawling over the seabed. Can you find them?

CORAL COLONIES

Corals may look like plants, but they are really colorful animals. They often live together in colonies. A coral reef is formed by millions of tiny creatures called polyps. The polyps build a coat of limestone around themselves, and when they die, other polyps build on top of them.

Soft corals look more like trees, with stems and branches that are strengthened by a chalky, often red or pink substance. The soft corals extend their colored tentacles to feed.

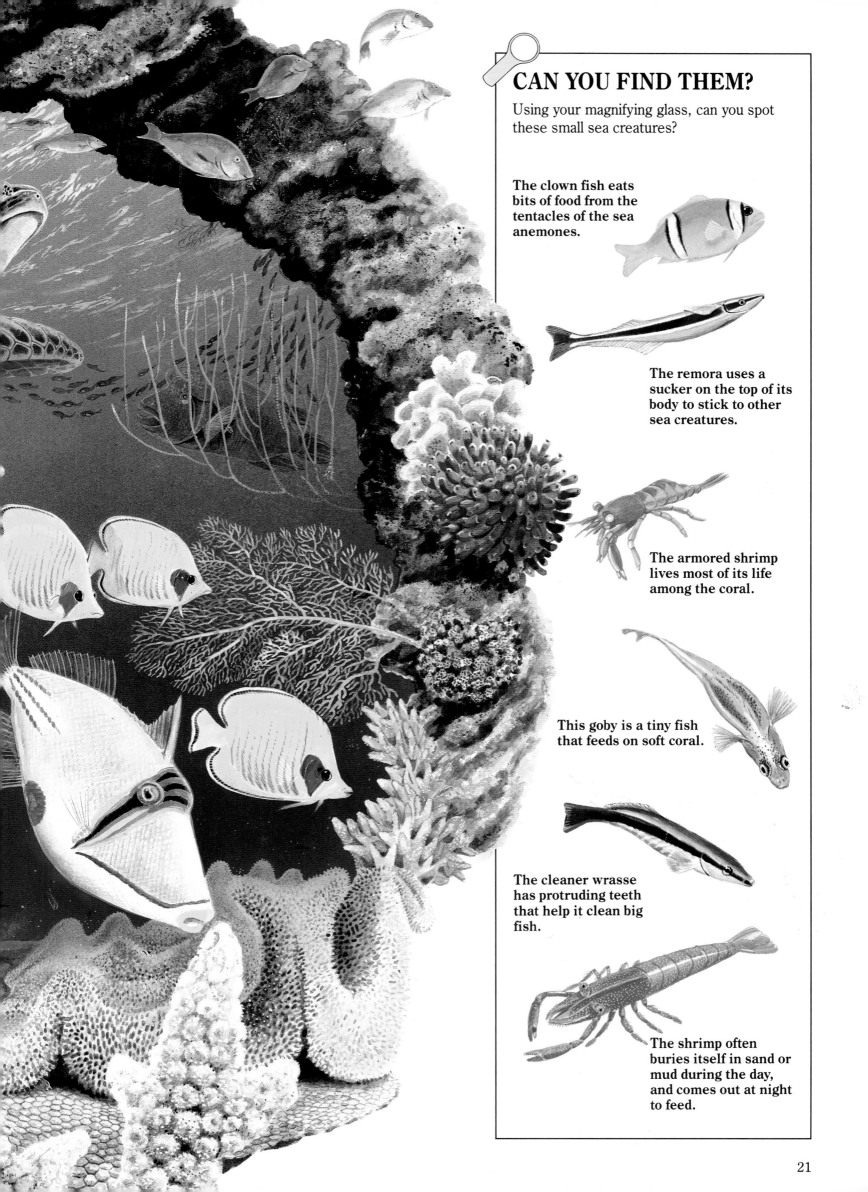

CAN YOU FIND THEM?

Using your magnifying glass, can you spot these small sea creatures?

The clown fish eats bits of food from the tentacles of the sea anemones.

The remora uses a sucker on the top of its body to stick to other sea creatures.

The armored shrimp lives most of its life among the coral.

This goby is a tiny fish that feeds on soft coral.

The cleaner wrasse has protruding teeth that help it clean big fish.

The shrimp often buries itself in sand or mud during the day, and comes out at night to feed.

PUZZLE ANSWERS

Most animals, just like people, have a special place where they can be safe. This is their home, where they can rest, sleep, and bring up their young. In the high mountains, big bears sleep through the winter in warm dens, and little marmots nest in cozy burrows. In the hot desert, coyote pups live in dens too. For them, their homes provide cool shade and protection.

Many birds build nests in trees, where they lay their eggs and raise their chicks. Kingfishers live in holes in the riverbank, and seabirds nest on rocky cliffs and ledges. Some desert birds, such as the elf owl and the woodpecker, even nest inside cacti.

Animals like frogs and newts live only in the water as tadpoles, then grow into adults that can live on land. Some creatures, such as the turtle and the cowry, have their own shells for homes. Vampire bats and other animals live in large groups or colonies; some, like the termites in this book, create amazing structures to call home.

Did you find all the hidden animals with your magnifying glass? In the following pictures, the position of each hidden animal is indicated by a circle. Answers to the puzzles are given as well.

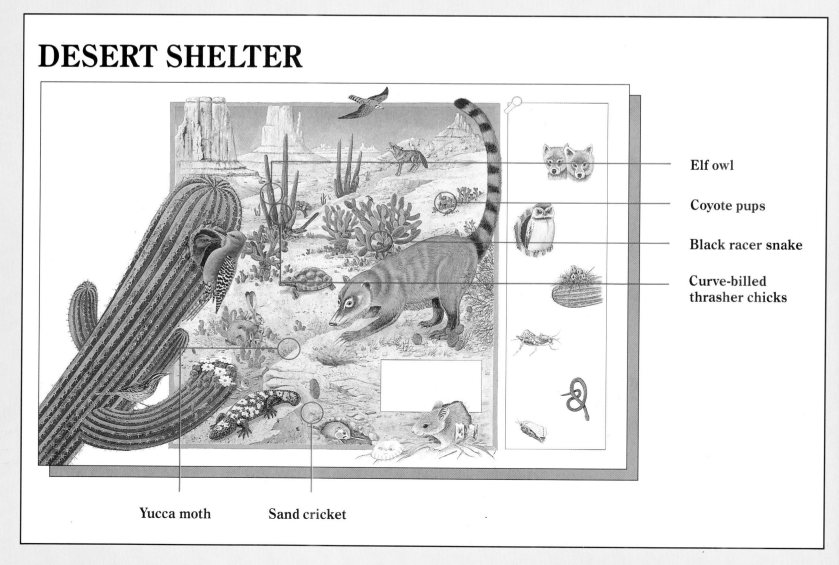

DESERT SHELTER

Elf owl

Coyote pups

Black racer snake

Curve-billed thrasher chicks

Yucca moth

Sand cricket

HIGH-RISE HOMES

Lesser black-backed gull egg

Guillemot egg

Kittiwake chicks

Kittiwake egg

Guillemot chick   Fulmar chick   Razorbill chick   Razorbill egg

RIVER HOMES

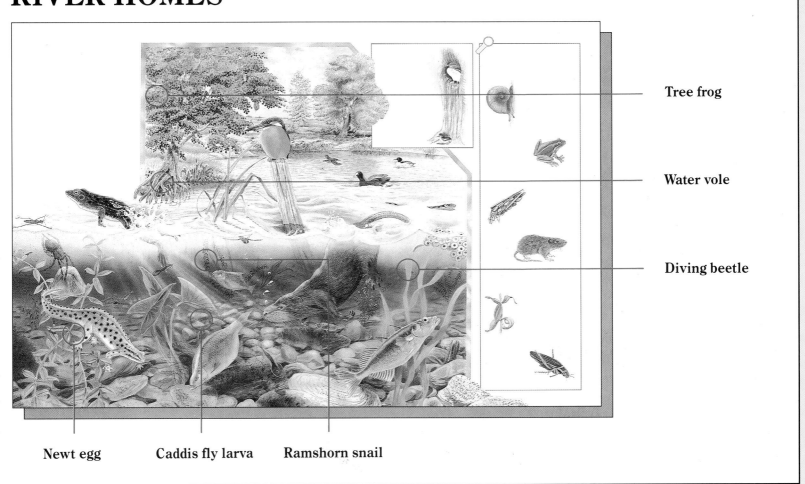

Tree frog

Water vole

Diving beetle

Newt egg   Caddis fly larva   Ramshorn snail

LEDGES AND CRAGS

Lammergeier nest

Alpine accentor nest

Wall creeper nest

Alpine chough nest

Rock nuthatch nest

SPOT THE DIFFERENCE

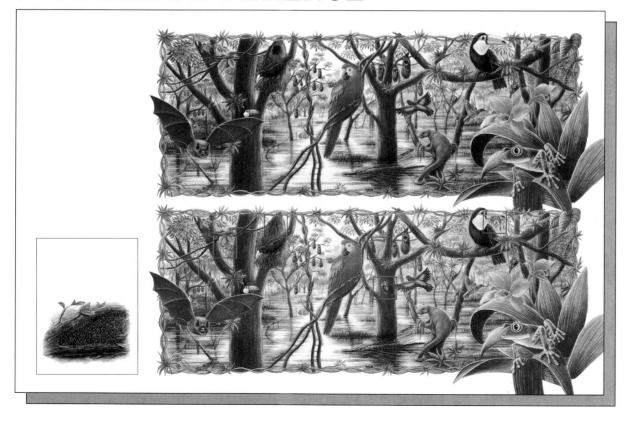

The differences are shown by ☐ .

MOUNDS AND BURROWS

This is the route the termite should take.

LIVING IN THE SEA

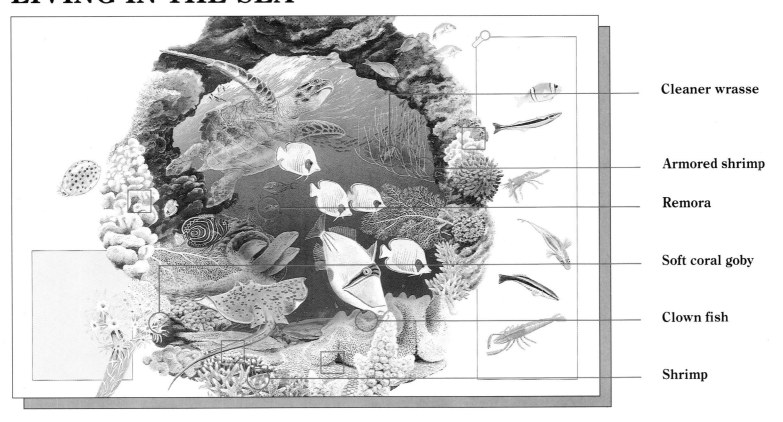

Cleaner wrasse

Armored shrimp

Remora

Soft coral goby

Clown fish

Shrimp

The cowries are shown by ☐ .

GLOSSARY

DESERT SHELTER
pages 8–9

American kestrel
The American kestrel is a small falcon that hovers in the air and swoops down on small mammals on the ground.

Black racer snake
The black racer snake is not poisonous but pins its prey to the ground.

Cactus wren
The cactus wren is a small bird that feeds on insects and seeds.

Coati
The coati is related to the racoon. Its young are born in tree nests, and females and their young live in groups.

Coyote
The coyote makes a den with a long tunnel and a nesting chamber.

Curve-billed thrasher
Thrashers are North American songbirds with curved bills and long tails.

Desert tortoise
The desert tortoise shelters in a burrow in the ground during the hottest part of the day.

Elf owl
The little elf owl is only about 5 inches tall. It nests in holes made by woodpeckers in cacti.

Gila monster
The gila monster is a large, poisonous lizard. It hunts prey by ''smelling'' with its tongue.

Gila woodpecker
The gila woodpecker nests in holes that it makes in cactus plants.

Jackrabbit
Jackrabbits are actually hares. They rarely drink, getting all the moisture they need from plants.

Kangaroo rat
Kangaroo rats can leap like kangaroos on their very long hind legs. They carry food in their large cheek pouches.

Pack rat
The pack rat usually comes out at night to look for food – and for shiny, discarded objects!

Roadrunner
Roadrunners are relatives of the cuckoo. They can run fast, reaching speeds of almost 25 miles an hour.

Sand cricket
This cricket is a large grasshopper that burrows in the sand.

Yucca moth
The yucca moth transfers pollen from one yucca flower to another.

HIGH-RISE HOMES
pages 10–11

Cormorant
Cormorants rarely fly far out to sea, but they are expert divers and swimmers and feed mainly on fish.

Fulmar
Fulmars are found in the Arctic and northern Pacific oceans, as well as in the Atlantic. They have silvery-gray wings.

Great black-backed gull
The great black-backed gull is much bigger than the lesser black-backed gull, and it has pink legs.

Guillemot
The guillemot stands upright, rather like a penguin. Its black neck and throat turn white in winter.

Herring gull
One of the most common gulls, the herring gull will eat almost anything. It is often seen inland.

Kittiwake
Kittiwakes spend most of their time out at sea, feeding on fish and other sea creatures. They come ashore to breed.

Lesser black-backed gull
The lesser black-backed gull is a common coastal gull with yellow legs.

Peregrine
The peregrine is a large falcon. It is one of the world's fastest creatures, diving from great heights at up to 215 miles an hour!

Puffin
Puffins use their wings to swim underwater when they are catching fish.

Rabbit
Rabbits live in burrows dug into the grassy cliff tops.

Razorbill
The razorbill is named after its big, sharp bill, which it uses to catch fish.

Seal
Common seals live near coasts and rarely swim far out to sea. Their pups are born on land in sheltered coves.

Shag
The shag is also called the green cormorant. It has glossy, bottle-green plumage.

RIVER HOMES
pages 12–13

Bream
The freshwater bream belongs to the carp family of fish. It lives in slow-moving rivers and lakes.

Caddis fly larva
Caddis flies are mothlike insects. Their larvae live in water.

Coot
The coot is a dark-colored bird that nests among tall water plants.

Diving beetle
The diving beetle has broad, fringed legs that help it swim and dive.

Dragonfly
Dragonflies have long, slender bodies and two pairs of wings. Their larvae, called nymphs, live underwater.

Goosander
The goosander eats fish and other freshwater animals. It has a pointed bill, with "teeth" that help it hold fish.

Grass snake
Grass snakes are often found in and around water. They feed on frogs, toads, and fish.

Kingfisher
Kingfishers use their long, pointed beaks to catch fish and build burrows in riverbanks, where they nest.

Marsh frog
The marsh frog, which can grow up to 6 inches long, is an active singer throughout the day and night.

Muskrat
Muskrats are large rodents that nest in tunnels dug into riverbanks. They are well adapted to living in water.

Penduline titmouse
The penduline titmouse feeds on insects in summer and seeds in winter.

Pond skater
The pond skater is a water bug that skims over the surface of the water.

Ramshorn snail
The ramshorn is a freshwater snail. Its name comes from the shape of its shell.

Smooth newt
The smooth newt is mainly olive-brown, with darker spots on its upperside.

Tadpole
A tadpole is the larva of a frog, toad, or newt. Tadpoles grow legs and turn into adult amphibians.

Three-spined stickleback
The three-spined stickleback has long spines on its back. The male fish builds the nest and defends it against any rival males.

Tree frog
Tree frogs live in marshes and damp woodlands. In spring they make their way to ponds and rivers to breed.

Water boatman
The water boatman is a bug with a flat body. It feeds mainly on water plants.

Water spider
The water spider lives underwater most of the time, breathing air trapped in its bell-shaped silk nest.

Water vole
Voles belong to the same family as mice. Although the water vole does not have webbed feet, it swims well.

Alpine accentor
In winter, alpine accentors often move down to lower slopes in family groups and small flocks.

Alpine chough
Alpine choughs belong to the crow family. They live in flocks made up mainly of pairs.

Blue sheep
The blue sheep, or bharal, is hunted by the snow leopard. Mothers take their lambs to high ledges in an attempt to keep them safe.

Brown bear
The Himalayan brown bear has a heavy undercoat in winter, when it hibernates in its den. Cubs stay with their mother for four to five years.

Ibex
The ibex is a wild mountain goat. It has massive, curved horns and is very nimble on rocks and crags.

Impeyan pheasant
The impeyan pheasant is a large mountain bird with glistening, rainbow-colored plumage.

Lammergeier
The lammergeier is also called the bearded vulture because of the tufts of feathers around its bill. It spends most of the day flying.

Leopard cat
The leopard cat is about the same size as a domestic cat. This forest animal feeds on birds and small mammals.

Marmot
A marmot is a small burrowing rodent. The Himalayan marmot is a relative of the North American prairie dog.

Musk deer
Unlike other deer, musk deer have no antlers. Males have long upper teeth, which they use as weapons.

Rock nuthatch
Nuthatches are songbirds with strong feet and bills. They open nuts with their bills.

Snow leopard
The snow leopard has a thick, spotted coat. It is a relative of the common leopard.

Wall creeper
Wall creepers are both graceful fliers and excellent rock climbers.

Armored shrimp
The pink armored shrimp feeds, mates, and lays its eggs on sections of coral.

Blue-spotted stingray
Stingrays are relatives of sharks. They carry their sting in a spine on their whiplike tails.

Butterfly fish
The butterfly fish has a deep, flat, brightly colored body and brushlike teeth.

Carpet sea anemone
Sea anemones have tentacles armed with stinging cells. The tentacles catch food and carry it to the mouth.

Cleaner wrasse
The cleaner wrasse will often station itself near a brightly colored sea anemone so that big fish will know where to find it.

Clown fish
The clown fish is covered in mucous that protects it from the anemone's sting.

Coral
Corals are tiny animals with stinging cells on their tentacles.

Cowry
Cowries are sea snails with colorful shells. They feed on tiny sea animals and plants.

Hawksbill turtle
The hawksbill turtle is a small sea turtle with a hooked, beaklike mouth.

Humphead
The humphead is a large, heavy-bodied fish.

Imperial angelfish
The imperial angelfish is a brightly colored fish that can grow up to 16 inches long.

Long-nosed parrot fish
A parrot fish has a ''beak'' formed by its fused teeth, which it uses to eat corals and sea plants.

Moray eel
The moray eel has a large mouth full of sharp teeth. It likes to lurk in crevices and holes, waiting to catch passing food.

Picasso triggerfish
If attacked by bigger fish, the triggerfish dives into corals and uses a special spine on its fin to ''lock'' itself into a safe position.

Remora
The remora has a sucking disc on its head that it uses to attach itself to larger sea creatures.

Sea slug
Sea slugs are sea snails without shells.

Shrimp
Shrimp are small crustaceans related to crabs and lobsters. They are found in both fresh and salt water in most parts of the world.

Soft coral goby
Soft coral gobies are colorful little fish. Their eyes are very close together on top of their heads.